THE SIMPLE ART O

JAPANESE
PAPERCRAFTS

THE SIMPLE ART OF

JAPANESE PAPERCRAFTS

35 GIFT IDEAS FOR
STEP-BY-STEP ORIENTAL STYLE

MARI ONO

CICO BOOKS
London

First published in 2006 by Cico Books Ltd
32 Great Sutton Street London EC1V 0NB

10 9 8 7 6 5 4 3 2 1

A CIP catalogue record for this book is available from
the British Library

ISBN 1 904991 34 3

Translated by Yukiko Tagawa
Support and consulting by Chizuko Tokuno and
      Natsuko Watanabe
Edited by Robin Gurdon
Photographs by Geoff Dann
Design by Christine Wood
Styling by Georgina Harris

Printed and bound in China

DENKIGASA—LAMPSHADE page 118:
Take care when you make this project; only use reputable
ready-made light fittings and very low-wattage bulbs, and
never allow the paper to touch a lit bulb.

CONTENTS

INTRODUCTION

After the introduction of papermaking to Japan from China in the sixth century AD, papermaking underwent a rapid change in both technique and the raw materials used, so creating unique Japanese paper, or *washi*. *Washi* is thin, durable, flexible, and insect resistant, and above all, beautiful. Because of the interplay of these characteristics with the Japanese style of life, it is still used in many aspects and occasions of life in Japan. As well as being the ideal medium for writing, painting, and printing, it is used in the home to make partitions such as sliding doors and screens, lighting covers for lanterns and lamps, and fans. It is also commonly used in hobbies and amusements such as paper folding, doll making, and card games, as well as wrapping.

Traditionally, hats were made from shiftu—fabric woven with thread twined with split washi. Now, washi can be processed into hats and dresses without the extra processes of spinning and weaving. These hats are light, durable, and waterproof.

Among these, what attracts me most is the Japanese craft of paper folding, or *origami*. It needs no special tools, studio, or equipment. Everyone, from children to adults, can enjoy making almost anything with just a single piece of paper. The fun you have as you fold the creases step by step, and the surprise that you get when you have finished, is like magic. You can then go on to enjoy the variety of impressions you can create through using combinations of different colors and types of paper.

The surfaces of this calendar have been scattered with seasonal flowers made from washi. The warm, light, hand-made touch of washi makes them especially popular.

Modern washi is used to make kyokarakami—envelopes for gifts of money—and karakami coasters. These new products have been designed by traditional washi studios in the styles of today, in the hope of spreading the use of washi through modern life.

Paper folding for amusement started sometime in Japan's Edo period (1603–1867) and has since been handed down from generation to generation. It once fell out of fashion but has now been revived as a figurative art, as part of the teaching materials at kindergartens and schools, for rehabilitation for people of advanced years, and, of course, as amusement for everybody.

But what I like best is that you can fold your sincerity into the product you are making. It can convey your warmth whether as a gift, a gift wrapper, or as a decoration in your house.

In this book, I have introduced some of the simple traditional folding designs, gift boxes, and stationery useful in our everyday life, along with guides for their creation. I have used Japanese paper for all work in this book, but you can make the projects even with non-Japanese papers. Get your favorite paper and enjoy making Japanese papercrafts.

Cards decorated with origami cranes are often folded as the token of a wish or the symbol of a prayer.

Origami is now available in many beautiful color tones.

All the Japanese paper in this book can be purchased. For more details, refer to the Suppliers directory on page 126.

THE HISTORY OF JAPANESE PAPERCRAFTS

Papermaking was invented in China at the beginning of the second century AD and was first brought into Japan, some 400 years later, subsequent to the introduction of Buddhism in the sixth century AD. As part of the efforts to disseminate Buddhism, and for official use, the government encouraged paper production for the transcription of sacred sutras.

The paper first brought into Japan was weak, easy to split and not insect resistant, making it difficult to preserve. As the demand for the production of more and better paper grew, *gampi*, a plant of the Daphne family indigenous to Japan was found to be an ideal raw material for paper. This prompted the Japanese to part ways with the original Chinese manufacturing method and led to the creation of Japanese paper—*washi*. Also, by the late 8th century, a new method of making paper from hemp and *kozo* (a plant of the Mulberry family), which adds the viscous mucilage of *tororo-aoi* (a plant of the Mallow family) was established. This is called the *nagashizuki* method. This development allowed the production of unusually thin, strong, and resistant paper with a minimal waste of natural resources.

At the outset of Japan's Heian period (794AD–1192), the regions of Japan became known for their own particular types of paper. Even today, these papers are preserved in impeccable condition in museums and private collections. When first produced, paper was used only for official documents and the transcription of religious texts because of its

Japanese chiyo origami is popular worldwide because of the variations of color and design. The impression given by an item changes with the design of the paper, making this paper one of the musts of origami handiwork.

THE MAKING OF JAPANESE PAPER

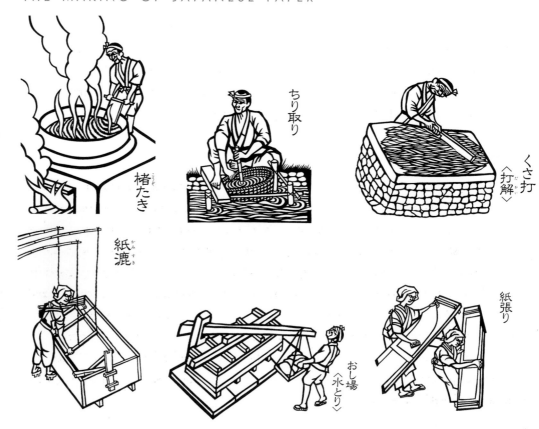

楮たき

ちり取り

くさ打
〈打解〉

紙漉

おし場
〈水とり〉

紙張り

The traditional papermaking process began with the boiling of the hemp or gampi. Excess flecks were then removed before the pulp was beaten flat. The pulp was then evenly laid out on wooden boards, and pressed, using rocks as weights. The sheets were then removed and left to dry.

scarcity and value. But increased production of quality paper soon prompted it to be used for private correspondence and poetry, and hence promoted the development of literature and art. *The Illustrated Handscroll Tale of Genji* (1120–40), is one of such early masterpieces. The original novel, written by Murasaki Shikibu early in the eleventh century, was painted into hand scrolls.

In medieval Japan, paper was still very valuable, but it soon became useful in various parts of everyday life. Good examples of this include *shoji*, the paper sliding screen, and *fusuma*, the paper sliding door. Especially during the Edo period (1603–1867), when Japan enjoyed a time of peace, paper was used in various necessities from *chochin* (lanterns), and *sensu* (folding fans), to *kamiko* (robes), and even *kappa* (raincoats).

Light and durable washi can make a beautiful folding fan.

The Birth of Origami

The origin of *origami* is not clear. It is said that one of the earliest instances of *origami* was decorative paperwork used in the Shinto ceremonies. Paper being a valuable commodity, it was regarded as divine and nobles would exchange letters or gifts attached with a cut paper now known as a *noshi*. In the *samurai* society, traces of *origami* could be seen in their special style of wrapping developed during the Muromachi period (1338–1573). But what is quite clear is that in the Edo period, when paper production increased massively, it became widely popular among ordinary townspeople. *Origami* cranes and various types of boat designs became popular as decorations on clothing, and are depicted in *ukiyoe* wood prints. The world's oldest paper-folding text book, *Hiden Senbazuru Orikata* (The Secret of One Thousand Origami Cranes) (1797) describes how to create many cranes connected together. This was followed by *Kayaragusa* (1845), which provides a comprehensive collection of *origami* models. Recreational *origami* developed as an amusement and method of decoration throughout society.

Washi Joins the World

After a long period of seclusion from the world, Japan relaxed her isolation in 1853. In 1873, at the Vienna World Exposition, Western people were surprised to see various commodities made of paper, such as parasols, rain umbrellas, folding fans, and fabrics made from *shifu*, which were exhibited by Japan. For Westerners, paper was merely a medium of writing, painting, and printing. *Washi*'s thin and soft but resilient characteristics enabled the Japanese to use it in various ways from daily necessities to recreational and artistic use. *Washi* is now actively used in various categories of work: arts, crafts, bookbinding, graphic design, and interior design to name a few. *Origami* is not only a popular amusement among children but it has become a hobby for adults. It is used for recreational purposes, but there are now many *origami* creators whose works have even reached the level of fine art.

The unryushi used to make this washi letter set has thick dominant fibers on the surface, which gives a deep impression on those who receive the letter—the perfect material with which to convey your sincerest feelings.

TYPES OF JAPANESE PAPER — WASHI

There are many types of traditional Japanese papers, known in their native country as *washi*, which are available and easy to use for paper folding (*origami*) or paper crafts, but each type's suitability depends on its characteristics and composition. To ensure clarity, the Japanese names are used throughout this book as it is not always easy to translate the papers' names into English.

The Chinese character representing the word for "paper" can be read in three ways in Japanese: *kami*, *gami*, or *shi*. The use of each form depends on the sentence and surrounding words: *kami* is used only on its own, and simply means "paper." *Gami* and *shi* mean the same thing but are both used as descriptions when attached to other words. Which one is used depends on the form of the word to which it is joined.

PLAIN PAPERS

Danshi, or Ceremony Paper, and Taireishi

Danshi is a thick, elegant white paper with a furrowed or creped texture, and is made from the fibers of the *kozo*, or mulberry tree. It was originally used for formal letters and diplomas. Especially in the Heian period (794–1192), court ladies favored it when writing poems. It is now used to wrap gifts and for making envelopes to hold a gift of money at weddings and other special occasions, including New Year and funerals. *Taireishi* has short fibers of mulberry visible on the surface of the paper and is used to print formal letters and documents. It is made at Echizen, in the present day Fukui prefecture, which is especially famous for production of *washi*.

Momigami

Momigami is a Japanese *washi* paper that has been scrunched up. It is often used for doll-making and mounting paintings or calligraphy because it is thin but strong. It is also suitable for gift wrapping and *origami*. The image on this page is a variation of *momigami* called *habutaeshi*. The paper has both sides printed with different colors and designs to make a fashionable gift-wrapping paper.

Tengujoshi, Rakusuishi, and Unryushi

Each of these papers is extremely thin, made using the most sophisticated techniques. *Tengujoshi* was described as "thin as a mayfly's wing" but is nonetheless extremely strong. It was originally used for artists' tracing paper, block copy for woodblock prints, and backing paper. Currently, it is used for wrapping jewelry and pieces of fine art as well as for restoring cultural properties. The image also shows the thin papers known as *rakusuishi* and *unryushi*. Light filtering through these beautiful thin papers produces warmth and soft beauty. They are used for *shoji*, the translucent sliding screen and *chochin*, the Japanese lantern. Enjoy the delicate silky touch of these papers in wrapping.

Mingeishi

Mingeishi is a general term for handmade *washi* which were produced from the 1920s in various parts of Japan as a result of the Mingei (folk craft) movement lead by the philosopher, Muneyoshi Yanagi who especially appreciated the beauty of everyday items created by nameless artisans. Some of the *gampishi*, the traditional handmade paper dating back to ancient times, is also produced as a type of *mingeishi*. Most of the *mingeishi* are *kozo* papers made from mulberry which makes them strong and resistant to tearing. They are still used widely for daily items such as envelopes, *fusuma* (sliding doors) and book binding.

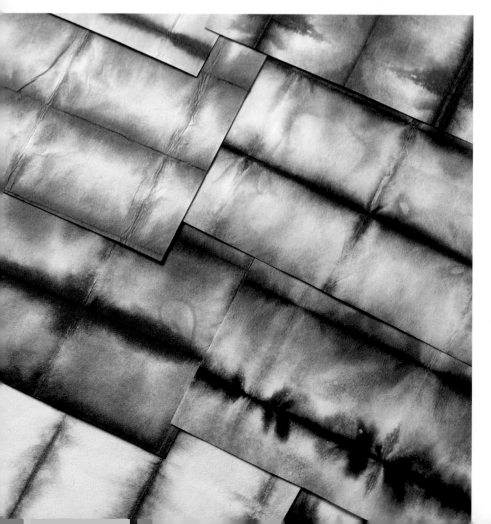

Itajimezomeshi

During the Edo period (1603–1867), people started making paper flowers for decoration at temples. To make them look more realistic, a paper dyeing method called *itajimezome* was invented. Two pieces of wood (*ita*) are wrapped with folded (*jime*) plain paper. They are clamped together, before part of the paper is dyed (*zome*), creating a pattern which repeats itself when the paper is unfolded. The design can differ according to the way the paper is folded. It is popular now for *origami* and gift-wrapping.

PATTERNED PAPERS

Kyo karakami

Karakami is made by printing designs with a woodblock stamp onto already beautifully dyed paper. The name originally referred to all the decorative papers imported from China in the Heian period (794–1192) that were used for painting and calligraphy. But they were soon imitated and produced in Japan. By the Muromachi period (1338–1573), strong and durable, yet decorative, *karakami* came to be used as *fusuma* (sliding doors) and *tsuitate* (screens), which were indispensable as partitions in houses built at that time. The paper shown here is made at the Karacho studio which was established during the Edo period. It is still used for *fusuma* at the Imperial Palaces as well as in high-grade interior decoration.

Kyo chiyogami

Chiyogami is a decorative paper that is either printed using woodblocks or, alternatively, colored in a method similar to that used for dyeing kimonos; the name *Kyo* refers to the region of Kyoto in which the paper is made. The designs are taken from various court nobles' patterns and kimono, or *yuzen*, patterns. Shown here are the traditional and chic small patterns of *kyo chiyogami* which are also suitable for *origami*.

Edo Chiyogami

Edo chiyogami is made in the Tokyo region and differs stylistically from *kyo chiyogami* by being more brightly colored and fashionable. *Chiyogami* originated in Kyoto, but when it was brought to Edo during the period in which Tokyo dominated the country it became linked with the woodblock printing technique of *ukiyoe*, and *chiyogami* with popular designs such as *kabuki* and *sumo* was produced. Nowadays, the paper is used as a material for handicrafts and various everyday items as well as interior decoration and stationery.

Sarasagami and katazomeshi

This is a stencil-dyed paper using patterns brought into Japan through trade with Spain and Portugal in the sixteenth century. Using *washi* laminated with persimmon tannin as the stencils, an Indonesian or other ethnic pattern is printed on the paper. It is used for handicrafts as well as *fusuma* and *shoji* in houses.

THE BASIC TECHNIQUES FOR ORIGAMI

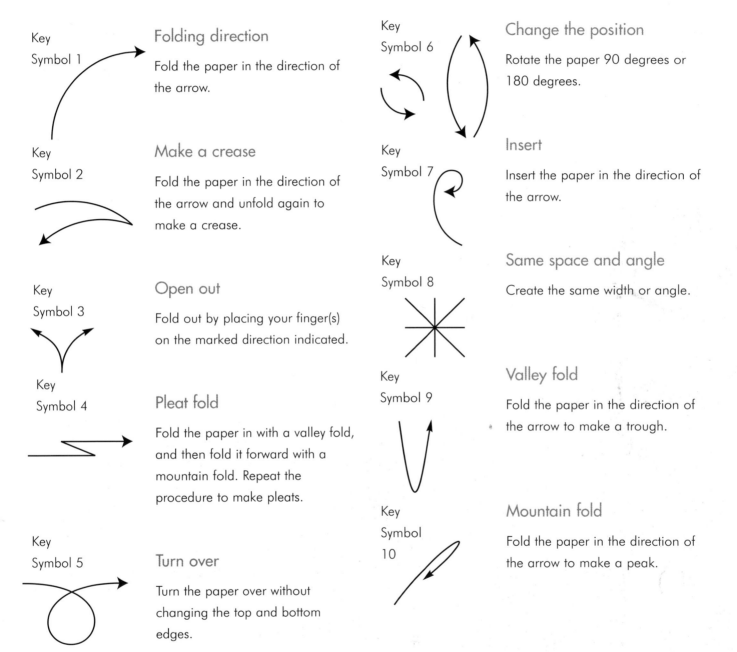

Key Symbol 1

Folding direction

Fold the paper in the direction of the arrow.

Key Symbol 2

Make a crease

Fold the paper in the direction of the arrow and unfold again to make a crease.

Key Symbol 3

Key Symbol 4

Open out

Fold out by placing your finger(s) on the marked direction indicated.

Pleat fold

Fold the paper in with a valley fold, and then fold it forward with a mountain fold. Repeat the procedure to make pleats.

Key Symbol 5

Turn over

Turn the paper over without changing the top and bottom edges.

Key Symbol 6

Change the position

Rotate the paper 90 degrees or 180 degrees.

Key Symbol 7

Insert

Insert the paper in the direction of the arrow.

Key Symbol 8

Same space and angle

Create the same width or angle.

Key Symbol 9

Valley fold

Fold the paper in the direction of the arrow to make a trough.

Key Symbol 10

Mountain fold

Fold the paper in the direction of the arrow to make a peak.

Difficulty level

The complexity of each project in the book has been calculated on a scale of 1–5. Level 1 is the simplest, while level 5 requires the use of some complex folding techniques. If you allow yourself to gain confidence gradually you will soon be successfully creating the most intricate of designs.

BASIC FOLDING TECHNIQUES

Square Fold

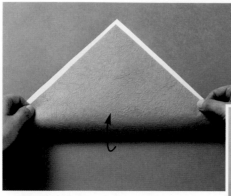

1 Fold a piece of square paper in half to make a triangle.

2 Fold it in half again.

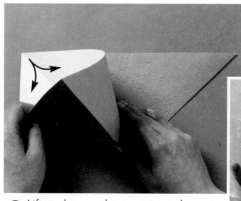

3 Lift and open the top triangular pocket, refolding it to make a square.

4 Turn the paper over and lift up the remaining triangular point.

5 Again, open out the fold and flatten it, to make a square.

Triangle Fold

1 Fold a piece of square paper in half to make a rectangle.

2 Fold it in half again to make a square.

3 Open out the top square pocket, refolding it to make a triangle.

4 Turn the paper over and lift the other square to the vertical.

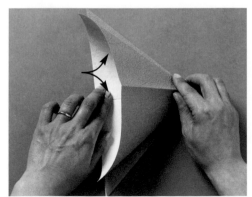

5 Open out the square, reshaping it to make a triangle as in step 3.

BASIC **ZABUTON**, OR FLOOR CUSHION SHAPE

1 Mark the center of a square piece of paper by lightly folding in half from corner to corner. Fold the first corner into the center.

2 Turn the paper through 90 degrees and fold the next corner into the center.

3 When all four corners have been folded in, the *zabuton* is complete.

A TIP FOR CUTTING PAPER

1 Mark the start and end points of your intended cut with an awl.

2 Set the metal edge of the ruler on the points marked in step 1. Cut along the ruler using the paper cutter. Be certain that the tip of the cutter follows the edge of the ruler.

A TIP FOR FOLDING THICK PAPER

1 Mark the starting and end points of your intended mountain fold with an awl. If you want to make a valley fold, make the crease for your intended fold on the reverse side of the paper.

2 Set the ruler on the points marked in step 1 and draw a line along the ruler using the awl, without cutting the paper. Make a mountain fold along the line you have drawn.

INSIDE FOLD

1 Following the dotted line in the diagram, make a crease at the tip of the triangle.

2 Unfold.

3 Open out the paper and fold the tip along the crease to make a mountain fold.

4 Make a valley fold between the mountain folds.

5 Fold the valley fold inside.

TRADITIONAL
PROJECTS

ORIZURU
CRANE

This the *origami* crane is perhaps the most famous design among the traditional Japanese paper-folding models it is also one of the most tricky. But, once you learn how to fold the crane, you should be able to make any design in this book. The crane has been regarded as a symbol of longevity in Japan since ancient times. You can make a nice greeting card by applying it as an accent, or use lovely paper to make it a gift in itself.

MATERIALS

◆ **1 sheet of *kyo-chiyogami* 7 x 7 in. (18 x 18cm)**

Difficulty level: 3

1 Begin with a square fold (see page 16). Fold the paper in half diagonally, then in half again to make a triangle.

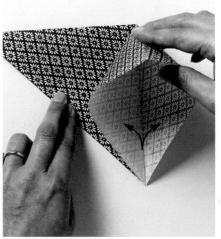

2 Open the upper pocket to make a square and flatten.

3 Turn the object over, and open out the pocket to make a square.

4 Fold the left and right flaps of the top layer into the center so that they meet in the middle.

5 Turn the object over, and repeat the previous step with the back flaps.

6 Fold the top triangle down to make a marker crease along the top of the folded flaps, and release.

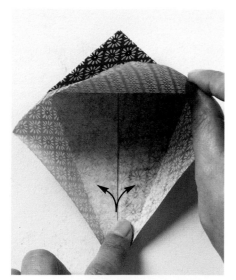

7 Open the outer flaps and use the marker crease from the previous step to lift the top layer of paper toward the top.

8 Push the far tip right of the diamond out so that the colored edges meet in the middle.

9 Turn the object over and repeat the previous two steps on the reverse so that you are left with a tall diamond-shaped object.

10 Fold the outer edges of both flaps on the top layer inward to meet at the center. Turn over and repeat with the reverse side.

11 Make marker creases at the top of both of the object's arms, and release.

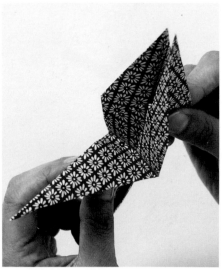

12 Open out the flap and make a reverse fold along one of the crease lines you have just made.

13 Close the flap around the folded up arm. Repeat the previous two steps on the other side.

14 Make a slanted fold halfway up one arm, unfold and fold it inside along the crease to make an inside fold for the crane's head.

15 Pull the wings downward and gently expand the crane's back to finish.

KUSU DAMA
DECORATIVE SPHERES

Inspired by Japanese *kusu dama*—hanging charms used to ward off sickness and evil spirits—these balls combine contrasting sheets of colored paper to create fun, decorative gifts. They have many possible uses: insert a bag of pot-pourri before you close up the ball to act as an air freshener, or enclose a bell to make a traditional Japanese baby's toy that will ring as a toddler rolls it about. Alternatively, to westernize the decoration, make the ball from shiny paper and hang it from a bouquet of flowers or a Christmas tree.

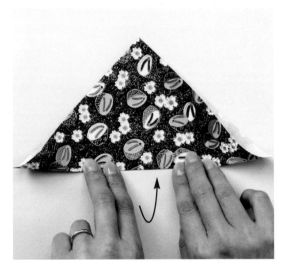

MATERIALS

◆ **6 sheets of *kyo chiyogami*, 6 x 6 in. (15 x 15cm)**

◆ **Paper glue**

◆ **Cocktail stick**

Difficulty level: 2

1 Take one piece of paper and fold it in half, making a diagonal crease from corner to corner. Open up and make a fold between the other two corners.

2 Fold one corner after another into the center, until you end up with another square.

3 Finish the square by folding in the final corner.

4 Turn over the paper and fold all the corners into the center.

5 Once again, turn the paper over and fold all the corners into the center.

6 Place a fingertip under one of the flaps at each corner and pull it open, creating a squared off arm at all four corners.

7 Repeat this whole process with five other sheets of paper. Begin joining them together by slotting one arm inside another.

8 Make permanent by using a cocktail stick to insert a little paper glue between the sheets at every joint.

9 Connect all the pieces of paper together until they lie flat in the shape shown above. If necessary, you can make a slight crease on the arm being inserted to help the fit.

12 Check that each join is equal, making an even sphere.

11 Complete the final link, finishing the ball, remembering to insert a bell or bag of pot-pourri now if you choose.

10 Turn over and begin slotting the remaining arms together, gluing each join in place with paper glue.

IRO BAKO—COLOR CUBE

Just as with the *kusu dama* (see pages 26–9), the color cube is created by combining six pieces of *origami* folded in the same way. You can make a cube by mixing and matching colors and designs in any way you like—you can even make color cubes of different sizes. One of the most traditional methods of folding *origami*, the cube can be given to children as a toy, or used as a room accessory. Alternatively, put some candy in it and use it as goodie bag at a children's party, or it could be a secret box to be sold at the fair.

MATERIALS

◆ **6 sheets of plain *mingeishi*, 6 x 6 in. (15 x 15cm)**

Difficulty level: 2

1 Take one sheet and fold in half to create the valley fold and unfold. Fold the top and bottom edges to the center. In this way, you have four vertical creases.

2 Unfold it again. Make a valley fold in the top left hand corner by folding the tip down to the nearest valley fold, then turn the paper round and repeat in what was the bottom right corner.

3 Fold the top and bottom edges in to the center fold.

4 Fold the bottom left corner up to the top edge and then hold it in place by slipping it under the top flap.

5 Turn the paper round and fold down the same corner before also putting it under the flap.

6 Turn it over, and fold both ends into the center to make a square. Release the points to leave two marker creases. The first piece is now complete.

7 Repeat steps 1 to 6 until you have made six pieces. Slot four of the pieces around the first by fitting the ends into the openings together in the pattern shown. Turn the combined papers over and lift the pieces up, slotting them together to make the sides of the box.

8 Fit the last piece in on the top as a lid, and fix it by guiding the box's two remaining ends into position.

TSUNOKOBAKO DECORATION BOX

This traditional *origami* design for holding sweets or trinkets, the *tsunokobako* is so simple that even a small child could make it. Like many of the most enduring *origami* designs, it has been handed down from mother to child. Here, the enchanting design of *chiyogami* is combined with plain *mingeishi*. Alternatively, you can make it with any size of paper or with a single piece of paper if you prefer.

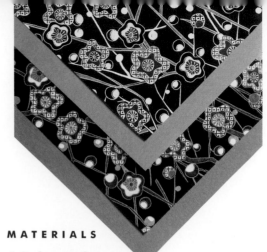

MATERIALS

◆ **2 sheets of origami (*edo-chiyogami* and *mingeishi*), 7 x 7 in. (18 x 18cm)**

◆ **Paper glue**

◆ **Cocktail stick**

Difficulty level: 2

1 Glue two sheets of paper together. Begin with a square fold then fold both sides back to the center. Turn over and repeat.

2 Rotate through 180 degrees and open out the pocket.

3 Fold the flaps in the direction of the arrows to make valley folds.

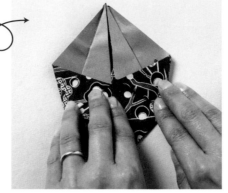

4 Turn over and repeat step 3.

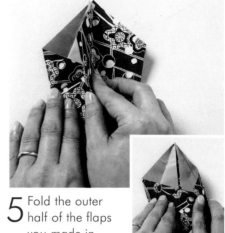

5 Fold the outer half of the flaps you made in steps 3 and 4 to the center to make mountain folds.

6 Turn over and do the same with the reverse side.

7 Turn down the center flap before repeating on the other side.

8 Fold the four upper tips down.

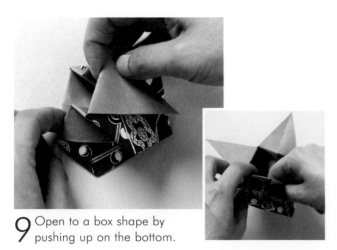

9 Open to a box shape by pushing up on the bottom.

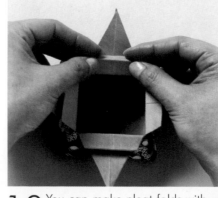

10 You can make pleat folds with the tips if you like.

FUSEN — BALLOON

Handed down from mother to child, there are many traditional *origami* models which are still being folded today. One of the oldest among them is this balloon. A single sheet of paper folds flat before being inflated with a single breath into a three-dimensional form to become a toy ball. This balloon will teach you the pleasure of *origami* folding—it is simple to make and you can increase your enjoyment of making it with different sizes and colors of paper. This is one of the magical *origami* models, dating from the days when there were not many toys for children to play with.

MATERIALS

◆ **1 sheet of *Edo-chiyogami*, 6 x 6 in. (15 x 15cm)**

Difficulty level: 2

1 Begin to create a triangle fold (see page 17) by making a pair of cross-shaped creases with valley folds.

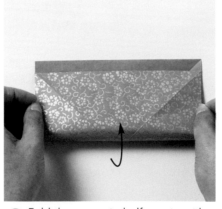

2 Fold the paper in half, again with a valley fold.

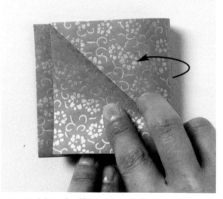

3 Fold in half again to form a square with a valley fold.

4 Open the upper pocket out into a triangle.

5 Turn over and lift the upper flap to the vertical.

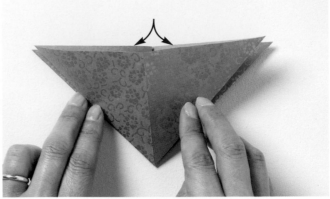

6 Press down, opening the pocket out into a triangle.

7 Fold the corners of the upper flap to meet the triangle's apex.

8 Turn over and repeat, folding the two corners to the apex to make a square.

9 Fold the right and left corners to the center with a valley fold.

10 Turn over and repeat the previous step.

11 Fold the upper tips of the top layer down toward the center to split a triangle in half, and repeat on the other side.

12 Fold the triangular shaped flap you just made and tuck it into the top pocket. Repeat this for the other side of the top layer, and for the reverse side.

13 Fold down the far tip and score the fold before releasing. Repeat on the reverse side.

14 Open the flaps out into a cross shape and blow gently through the hole, slowly inflating the balloon while easing out the creases.

KABUTO—SAMURAI HELMET

Every year in May the Japanese mark Children's Day. One of the ways of celebrating the healthy growth and development of boys is by decorating *kabuto*, or samurai helmets, a traditional *origami* design and miniature armor. We often make this *kabuto* with a sheet of newspaper for little children to wear. As it is simple to fold, you can enjoy making *kabuto* in the size of a child's hat, with the help of the child who will wear it.

MATERIAL

◆ **1 sheet of *edo-chiyogami*, 6 x 6 in.
(15 x 15cm)**

Difficulty level: 1

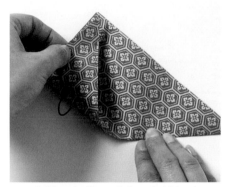

1 Fold in half, and then fold both corners of the triangle to meet at the bottom tip, creating a square.

2 Rotate the paper through 180 degrees and fold up the right and left flaps in half to meet at the top of the object.

3 Fold the top flaps away from the vertical center line, creating triangles.

4 Fold the upper flap of the bottom half away from you, leaving its tip about ⅝ in. (1.5cm) below the object's upper tip.

5 Fold the bottom of the flap made in step 4 away from you, using the center line as the crease line.

6 Turn and slide the bottom flap up inside the helmet to finish. Mount the hat on a stand or stick it to card to make an artwork.

TATO—CD HOLDER

Tato are age-old designs that were traditionally used as wallets to keep money, or containers to hold small items like needles and thread in the home. Of the many designs of *tato*, this is one of the simplest. Although it can be used as a coin purse or for wrapping small gifts, it is ideal for holding CDs or DVDs. To ensure you create a fine *tato*, use a resilient paper and make your creases neat and firm. When you have successfully made a *tato* with *washi* you can try your hand using various other types of paper.

MATERIALS

◆ **1 sheet of thick *unryushi*, 15 x 15 in. (38 x 38cm)**

Difficulty level: 3

1 Divide the paper into thirds and make creases using valley folds.

2 Unfold the paper and make two diagonal creases, corner to corner.

3 Unfold and turn the sheet 90 degrees before dividing the paper into thirds, at right angles to Step 1, and make creases.

4 Turn the paper over, and fold each corner two-thirds of the way toward its opposite, making the crease when the tip is level with the crossing of the folds nearest the corner.

5 Turn the paper back over. When all the creases have been made it should look like this.

6 Turn the paper over again. Hold the outside of two opposite corners and squeeze them together so that the sheet begins to fold, following the diagonal crease lines.

7 As the sheet folds in on itself, it begins to interlock in the center, leaving a four-pronged star shape.

8 This is the base on which to place the gift or CD. Now fold the flaps over one by one.

9 Finish by inserting the last flap into the pocket to close up the *tato*.

AYAME—IRIS

The traditional paper-folding design of the iris flower creates a solid and romantic piece. The secret of making a perfect iris is to ensure each corner is folded sharply, and to make sure the paper edges fit together neatly and tightly to within a hair's breadth. The final procedure of adding a curl on the petals makes a lovely flower. It may seem difficult at the beginning, but as there are many repetitive procedures in folding the iris, you will be successful after practicing a few times. Here I have made a series of iris flowers and put them in a glass vase—enjoy arranging them in your own original way.

MATERIALS

◆ **1 piece of *origami* for each flower 6 x 6 in. (15 x 15cm)**

◆ **A pencil or round stick**

Difficulty level: 5

1 Begin by making a square fold (see page 16). Fold one pocket over to make a crease. Unfold and open up the pocket and refold along the crease you just made.

2 Turn over and repeat on the other pockets to make a square.

3 Fold the left hand flap across the center and fold forward.

4 Turn the object over and repeat on the other side.

5 Fold one side of the small triangle into the middle.

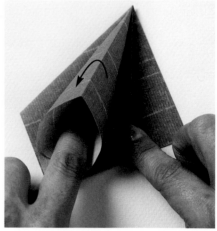

6 Open out the other flaps and repeat the previous step.

7 Rotate the object 180 degrees so that the divided flaps point away from you. Now fold the points back to meet at the bottom in the center, repeating this procedure on every flap.

8 Open these folds out and use them as marker folds, pushing down the lower part of the fold so that the paper meets along the vertical. Repeat on every flap.

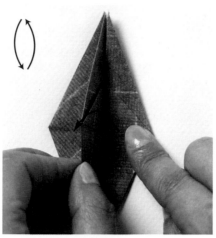

9 Fold up the bottom triangle of each of the four sections.

10 Turn the object back through 180 degrees and fold each flap in half.

11 Fold the outer edges of the top flap in to meet in the center. Repeat on the other flaps.

12 To open out the petals, fold down one end of each flap which was folded in the previous step.

13 When all four are bent over, curl down the tips of every flap with a pencil.

WATOJI BON—JAPANESE BOOKBINDING

Watoji is a traditional Japanese bookmaking method. During the Edo period (1603–1867) a boom in publishing books took place when the production of *washi* paper increased and woodblock printing developed. Craftsmen in Edo, present-day Tokyo, devised various types of bookbinding methods that made good use of their many techniques and styles. This particular technique is still used to produce various types of books and notebooks, such as a guest book used at a reception party. Fold the sheets of paper in half to make inner pages of double thickness, and bind at the edge opposite to the folded edge, enabling the paper to be inscribed or printed only on the facing surface of the paper, thus preventing blotting of the ink. The method is simple, and you do not need any special tools or techniques. If you use a beautiful *chiyogami* design for its cover, then you can create a traditional oriental flavor. You can even make your own original notebooks by using papers from around the world and applying ribbon and wool in place of the thread.

MATERIALS

- **24 sheets of calligraphy paper 13 x 9½ in. (33 x 24cm)**
- **2 sheets patterned *washi* for the cover 10½ x 14¼ in. (26.5 x 36cm)**
- **2 sheets *washi* for the inside backing of the cover 9½ x 6½ in. (24 x 16.5cm)**

- **Embroidery thread**
- **Paper glue**
- **Pasting brush**
- **Scissors**
- **Paper cutter**
- **Binder clip**

- **Ruler**
- **Needle**
- **Awl**

Difficulty level: 4

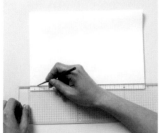

1 To bind the inner pages, fold each of the individual calligraphy papers in half. Take one and rule a line ½ in. (1.25cm) in from the loose edges. Mark two points on the line, ½ in. (1.25cm) from the top and bottom, and another two points to divide the line equally into three lengths.

2 Stack and clip the pages together along the folded length, protecting the pages from the binder clip with paper. Use an awl to perforate the pages at the central marks. With the thread for provisional binding, bind the stack tightly.

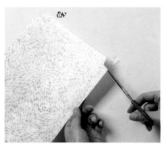

3 To make the cover, cut the paper to size, the height of the book plus 1 in. (2.5cm) and width plus 1¼ in. (3cm). Cut away the corners.

4 Fold the edges over to the marks cut out of the corners in the previous step.

5 Apply a light layer of water-thinned glue to the folded edges of the cover with a brush and stick on the backing paper of the cover.

6 Prepare the back cover in the same way and stack the covers and inner pages together and clip them. Use the awl to perforate the covers and thread twine to assemble the book.

7 Bind the whole book tightly following the order shown.

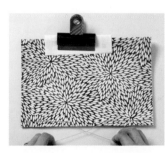

8 Make the knot either at the center, as here, or at the bottom edge, and tuck it into the hole.

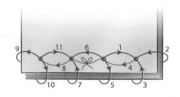

MONKIRIASOBI
PAPERCUTTING

Monkiriasobi combines the skills of *origami* and paper cutting. After folding, surprisingly beautiful designs can be made from cutting patterns into square paper. *Monkiriasobi* became widespread in Japan during the Edo period (1603–1867) when popular culture flourished in Japan. In particular, family crests called *kamon* and snow crystals were popular designs in those days. You can use your papercut pieces on accessories, coasters and ornaments in your room.

MATERIALS

◆ **1 sheet of *kozo*
  6 x 6 in. (15 x 15cm)**
◆ **Protractor**
◆ **Pencil**
◆ **Scissors**

Difficulty level: 2

1 Fold the paper in half to make a triangle, and use the protractor to fold the right corner up toward the top at an angle of 36 degrees.

2 Fold the right side again at the same angle, and fold the left corner along the crease you just made with the right corner.

3 Fold the left corner along the right edge to make a valley fold. At this stage ensure that the edges of the object align.

4 Lightly draw in the pattern you will cut with a pencil.

5 Cut along the lines of the design with scissors.

6 Open up the paper carefully, so as not to tear it.

SUIREN — WATER LILY

The water lily, or lotus flower, has long been beloved as the pure and sacred flower of Buddha. Although the traditional design of the water lily is simple, the finished flower is very pretty. Once you have learnt how to fold it, you can make it for your friends and children. You can arrange them on a flat plate or use the lotus leaf as a plate for sweets with which to entertain your guests.

MATERIALS

- ◆ 2 sheets of *itajimezomeshi*:
  6 x 6 in. (15 x 15cm) for the flower
  6 x 3 in. (15 x 7.5 cm) for the leaf

- ◆ Glue

Difficulty level: 3

LOTUS FLOWER

1 Begin by making the basic *zabuton*, or floor cushion shape (see page 18), and repeat.

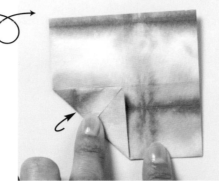

2 Turn over and again fold the four corners into the center.

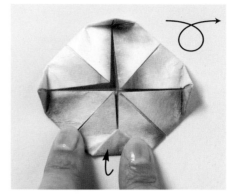

3 Fold in the tips of the four edges about ½ in. (1.25cm) to make valley folds.

4 Turn over. While holding the tips made in step 3, bring the tips of four flaps in the center to the reverse side.

5 Gently bring the four flaps to the reverse side and make them round with your finger.

6 Smooth out the base of the flower by pulling the tips while holding the flower.

LOTUS LEAF

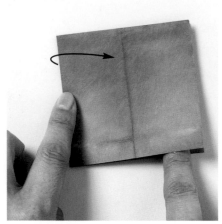

1 Make a horizontal crease in the middle of the paper.

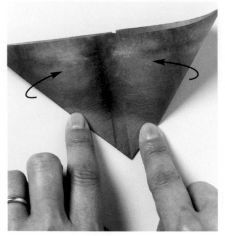

2 Fold both edges under to meet in the center on the reverse side.

3 Fold the right side of the triangle up to meet the center crease and open up the reverse side. Repeat the same procedure for the left side.

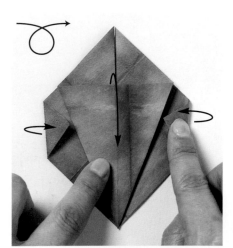

4 Turn over. Fold right and left corners in. Open the middle pocket to the center crease and fold it down as in the previous step.

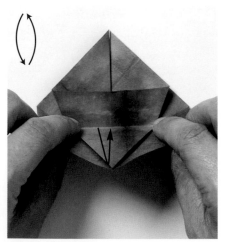

5 Spin the object through 180 degrees, then fold down the two tips from the top to make creases. Unfold.

6 Fold the tips inward.

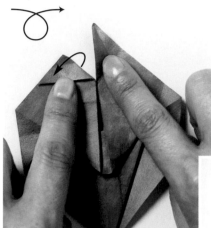

7 Turn over and fold back tips at the top away from the center.

8 Fold back the new topmost points.

9 Turn the leaf over and paste the lotus flower onto it at the pointed end of the leaf with glue.

GIFT BOXES AND
WRAPPERS

HAKO—SQUARE BOX

It is simple to create a gift box from just a single sheet of paper, with *origami* techniques that use neither scissors nor glue. Any paper will do, as long as you can divide it into two squares of similar, but not identical, size—from these you can make a gorgeous box with a lid. You can make any size of box; and even make boxes of different sizes and pile them into one another, one by one. Here, I used *washi* with a typical *aizome* design, a traditional dyeing method.

MATERIALS

◆ **2 sheets of *chiyogami*:**
 one size for lid depending on size of lid;
 one size for box depending on size of box
 (see table opposite)

Difficulty level: 2

	6 x 6 in. 15 x 15cm	8 x 8 in. 20 x 20cm	10 x 10 in. 25 x 25cm	12 x 12 in. 30 x 30cm
Paper size for lid	6 x 6 in. 15 x 15cm	8 x 8 in. 20 x 20cm	10 x 10 in. 25 x 25cm	12 x 12 in. 30 x 30cm
Size of lid	2¼ x 2¼ x 1 in. 5.5 x 5.5 x 2.5cm	3 x 3 x 1½ in. 7.5 x 7.5 x 3.5cm	3½ x 3½ x 1¾ in. 8.5 x 8.5 x 4.5cm	4½ x 4½ x 2¼ in. 10.5 x 10.5 x 5.5cm
Paper size for box	5½ x 5½ in. 14 x 14cm	7½ x 7½ in. 19 x 19cm	9 x 9 in. 24 x 24cm	11¼ x 11¼ in. 28.5 x 28.5cm
Size of box	2 x 2 x ⅞ in. 5 x 5 x 2.4cm	2½ x 2½ x 1⅜ in. 6.5 x 6.5 x 3.4cm	3¼ x 3¼ x 1⅝ in. 8 x 8 x 4.4cm	4 x 4 x 2⅜ in. 10 x 10 x 5.4cm

1 Make a cross-shaped crease, and fold each corner to the center to make the basic *zabuton* or floor cushion (see page 18). Precision at this stage will be helpful later.

2 Fold the top and bottom edges to the center to make valley folds before unfolding again to the shape of a *zabuton*.

3 Turn the paper through 90 degrees and make valley folds as in step 2 before again unfolding to a *zabuton* shape and opening out the top and bottom flaps as in the photo.

4 Taking two neighboring edges, make two sides of the box by lifting them toward the vertical. Ensure that the fold creating the corner of the box is inside the box. Fold the top flap back inside over the crease to make the corner of the box.

5 Repeat step 4 for the crease on the other side.

6 Fold the flap inside.

7 Repeat the whole process on the opposite side.

For the lid: refer to the table above for the paper sizes and make another box in exactly the same way but with slightly larger dimensions as described.

NAGA BAKO — RECTANGLE BOX

Just as you created a square box (see pages 58–9), here we will create a gift box of rectangular shape. A box made with *washi* or a n elegant gift wrap that you have to hand can add a unique touch to an ordinary gift. Your father may appreciate your Father's Day present even more when he finds a necktie in this handmade box. (Anyone who receives a gift in this handmade box may appreciate it even more.)

This box can be used not only as a gift box but also for keeping handy items, like your eye glasses, on the desk at home. If the box is to contain heavy items, apply cardboard to the bottom and four sides when folding the paper.

MATERIALS

◆ **2 sheets of *kyo-chiyogami*:**
   10 x 10 in. (25.5 x 25.5cm)
   for the box
   11 x 11 in. (28 x 28cm) for
   the lid

Difficulty level: 2

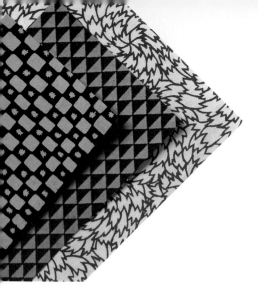

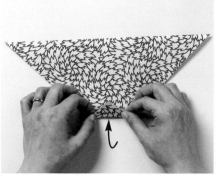

1 Fold the sheet in half diagonally. Mark the point ⅛ of the way from the tip to the fold line and make a crease.

2 Open out the paper. Fold top and bottom creases made in step 1 to make valley folds and then fold both sides into the center.

3 Fold the top and bottom flaps toward the center, making valley folds.

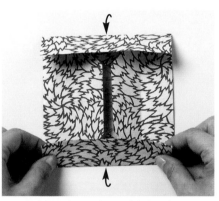

4 Fold in the right and left sides to make valley folds.

5 Fold the top and bottom sides into the center and unfold.

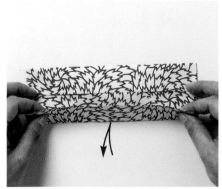

6 Turn the paper through 90 degrees and fold the top and bottom sides to make creases before unfolding the top and bottom corners.

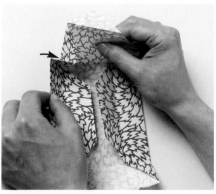

7 Fold the left horizontal crease to stand the left side upright and then fold the top flap inside to make the corner of the box. Repeat the step on the right side.

8 Fold the flap inside and do the same with the opposite side.

BARA ZUTSUMI—ROSE BOX

This is the perfect wrapping for a special gift such as a wedding present which uses textured paper such as *momiwashi* to produce a really exciting effect. By using soft but strong paper, you can make a pretty flower decoration, which is made by simply rolling up a thin strip of paper. As the flower can be used as a corsage or an accessory you will always find uses for it once you have learnt how to make it.

MATERIALS
◆ **1 sheet of *momiwashi* 18 x 18 in. (45 x 45cm)**
◆ **Paper string or ribbon**
◆ **2 strips of *momiwashi* 18 x 1¾ in. (45 x 4cm)**
◆ **Cocktail stick**
◆ **Thin wire**
The paper needed should measure twice the height and width of the box by twice its width

Difficulty level: 3

1 Place the box in the middle of the paper. While holding the box still, fold the bottom left corner of the *washi* up and over the center of the box.

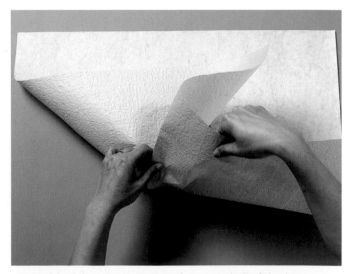

2 Holding the paper against the top edge of the box, wrap the box in a clockwise direction, folding each layer beneath the last as you move.

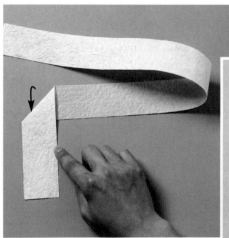

3 Continue to gather the tucks until you are holding all of them tightly together.

4 Tie the folds in place with paper string.

MAKING A ROSE

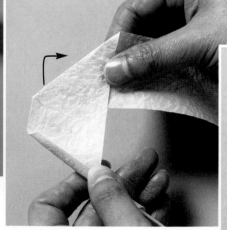

5 Make a right-angled valley fold in one of the long strips of *washi* 2 in. (5cm) from one end.

6 To make the flower stem use a cocktail stick as a core to roll the paper up on itself.

7 Continue rolling through the turn, so the paper's plain back is visible alongside the colored front.

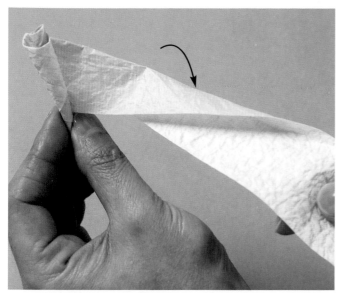

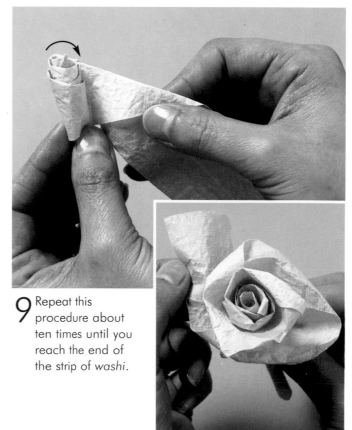

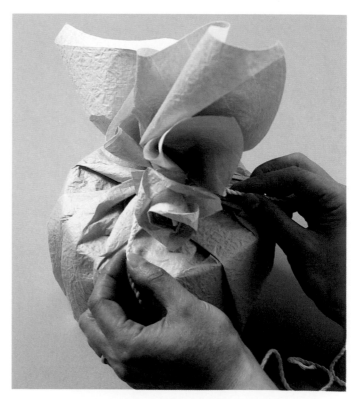

8 While holding the stalk of the rose flower, make a mountain fold and continue rolling along the crease. You can remove the cocktail stick.

9 Repeat this procedure about ten times until you reach the end of the strip of *washi*.

10 Twist the stalk firmly, fold over the loose end and tie it in place with wire, leaving long ends.

11 Use the wire ends to attach the rose flower to the paper string holding together the sheet of *momiwashi*.

TATO BAKO—CAKE BOX

Perhaps the most important tip for creating a perfect gift box is to make neat and accurate creases. This box—a variation of the "*tato*" folds introduced on page 40—might seem a little complicated, but it needs extra care only in the last steps when assembling the box. You can make a box of any size depending on the size of the paper you have. It is advisable to use thick, firm paper. Here, I used modern *washi* with a cosmic design but you can have fun changing the design of paper to suit the occasion.

MATERIALS
◆ **1 sheet of modern *washi*
12 x 12 in. (30 x 30cm)**

Difficulty level: 5

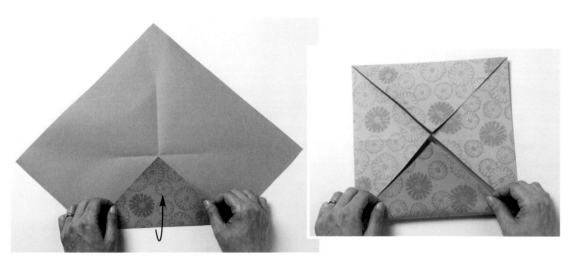

1 Make a cross-shaped crease, and fold each corner into the center to make the *zabuton* or floor cushion (see page 18).

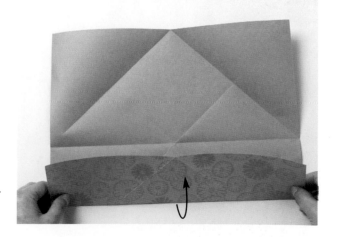

2 Unfold, and fold the top and bottom edges to the center to make valley folds. Unfold, rotate the paper 90 degrees and repeat.

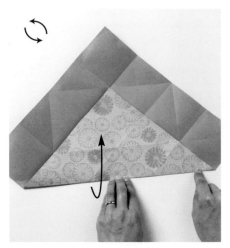

3 Rotate the paper 45 degrees and bring the bottom corner up toward the top point, folding it in line with the outer set of creases. Repeat at all four corners.

4 Make short valley folds across the squares nearest each corner. Make a sharp crease.

5 Fold the sheet over, placing the same marks together and make the creases across each corner.

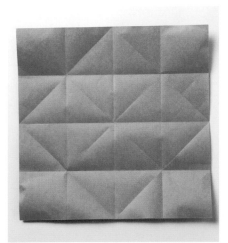

6 When all the creases across the corners have been made the sheet should look like this.

7 Turn the paper over again, and pinch together the crease at the top right.

8 Begin to stand the right edge up by turning the pinched edge up on itself.

9 Pinch the mountain fold at the adjacent corner and put the left flap over the right flap to create the first corner of the box.

10 While holding the corner with your right hand so as not to allow it to reopen, repeat the previous step to make the left corner.

11 When you are finished with the second corner, hold both corners and proceed with the third corner.

12 While keeping the top of the box together, fold the last corner and prepare to slot it into the top.

13 Finish by arranging the top of the box to look neat.

HANA BAKO
FLOWER BOX

This simply folded box can be used either as a flower vase or a flower pot if
made from a thick piece of paper with silver foil pasted inside as waterproofing,
and is ideal as a gift box for flowers to be given away at a wedding. Continue the floral theme by making
the box from handmade *washi* paper with real leaves and flowers scattered over the surface. Because of
the thickness of the paper, you could also make a matching greetings
card, or gift box.

MATERIALS

◆ **1 sheet of thick**
   washi **paper,**
   12 x 12 in.
   (30 x 30cm)

◆ **Glue**

Difficulty level: 1

1 Make mountain folds from corner to corner, then open out and repeat on the other diagonal. Open the sheet out again and half it with valley folds top-to-bottom, and side-to-side.

2 Pick up the paper and squeeze it together into the square.

3 Mark a point ¾ in. (2cm) from the bottom, fold the tip up and score.

4 Mark 1½ in. (3.5cm) from the far tip and fold the upper flap forward, then turn the object over and repeat.

5 Fold both upper flaps together so that their tips meet in the center. Turn over and repeat on the object's other side.

6 Paste the flaps to both sides of box. Unfold.

7 Raise the folded flaps and open the box by prising it open from the inside. Fold four corners at the top to make mountain folds.

8 Gently flatten out the bottom of the box to give the box its final shape.

HANA ZUTSUMI—FLOWER WRAPPER

Use paper and ribbon of your own choosing to enjoy wrapping flowers into personal bouquets. Here, I used *rakusuishi*—its thin but resilient characteristics give the delicate and elegant finish which are also ideal for giftwrapping a bottle (see pages 74–5). If you prefer to use very thin or light colored paper, put a few sheets together to give it strength; reversible or thick paper may give a different impression. Always try to use wrapping that enhances the flowers' beauty, so ensuring you have a bouquet which looks pretty when seen from every angle.

MATERIALS

- ◆ 1 sheet of rectangular *rakusuishi* (A) 1½ times the length of the bouquet by its length
- ◆ 1 sheet of square *rakusuishi* (B) the length of the bouquet
- ◆ Two pieces of ribbon
- ◆ String
- ◆ Scissors

Difficulty level: 1

1 Choose which color you want as the inner layer. Cut this sheet into a square (sheet B) and after turning it through 45 degrees lay it over one end of sheet A as shown in the photo.

2 To keep the paper dry, wrap the base of the bouquet in foil. Place it on the paper so that it is framed by sheet B. Cover the stems of the bouquet by folding up the bottom flap of sheet A.

3 While holding the bottom of the bouquet, bring the right side of paper toward the center without covering the bouquet entirely and score the edge.

4 Starting from the center, lightly fold the paper back at an angle to the stalks. Score this fold and tuck in an extra, small fold.

5 Repeat the process, making further, smaller folds fanning out from the middle, remembering to score all the folds.

6 Repeat steps 3 to 5 on the left hand side of the bouquet, mirroring the folds you have already made before fixing the paper in place around the stalk near the bottom with a string.

7 To hide the string, tie a ribbon over it around the bouquet and fix in a bow.

8 To give your bouquet a balanced look make adjustments if needed and unfold any paper which has become overlapped.

BIN ZUTSUMI
BOTTLE WRAPPING

It is common across the world for people to select gifts to show their own feelings whatever the occasion. Whether it is to mark a happy occasion or is intended to show respect, love, or condolence, the presentation of such a gift requires a special touch. Specifically, every present deserves a special wrapping. *Rakusuishi*, an extremely thin Japanese paper noted for its durability and gorgeous appearance, is the perfect material and this bottle-wrapping method takes only minutes to complete.

MATERIALS

◆ **1 sheet of *rakusuishi*, 15 x 24 in. (38 x 61cm)**

◆ **Paper string, or ribbon**

Difficulty level: 2

1 Work out the width of the paper required by measuring the height of the bottle, doubling it and adding the diameter of the bottle's base. Place the bottle in the center and begin to wrap by lifting the near right corner of the paper against the bottle.

2 Holding the paper against the bottle with your left hand, make the first crease of the wrapping by pulling the paper's top edge forward over the paper being held against the bottle.

3 Move the thumb up the bottle, holding the folds in place, and continue to make creases.

4 Repeat until all the paper available on the right is being held against the bottle.

5 Now, holding the creased paper against the bottle with the right hand, fold the remaining paper against the bottle, repeating the previous steps in reverse, using your left hand.

6 When complete, hold the paper against the neck of the bottle and even out all the folds around the back of the bottle.

7 Holding the paper with your left hand, wrap some string three or four times around the neck of the bottle.

8 Tie the string in place with an ordinary bow.

HASHI BUKURO
CHOPSTICKS WRAPPER

Wrapping chopsticks in paper can add an Asian flair to your oriental-style home party. Chopstick wrappers were originally made by Japanese chefs to accompany the meal. In the home, chopstick wrappers were, and still are, used on special occasions, such as New Year's Day, and decorated with the names of family members. Here, I used thin and easy-to-fold *kozo* paper. To finish your table setting, put the sharp end of the chopsticks inside the wrapper, with the handles extending out of the wrapper.

MATERIALS

◆ 1 sheet of *kozo*, 7 x 12 in. (18 x 30cm)

◆ *Kozo* decorations cut in the shape of cherry flowers and maple leaves

◆ Glue

◆ Cocktail Stick

Difficulty level: 1

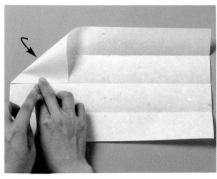

1 Fold the paper in half and then each half again into the center to make marker creases. Unfold and turn the top left corner down to the center crease.

2 Start folding from the bottom up into the center, making valley folds, and continue until the object is the width of one fold.

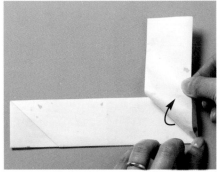

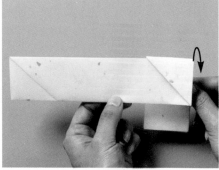

3 Turn over the end, marking the crease when the turned end is level with the visible edge of the turned corner.

4 Fold back the plain end, turning it at right angles and making a mountain fold.

5 Lift the paper and wrap the tail once around the bottom of the object.

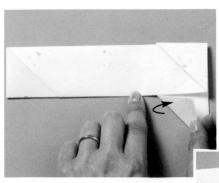

6 Fold the end of the tail into a triangle along the side of the object before turning the end over and tucking it in place.

7 Fold a cherry flower or maple leafaround the edge of the wrapper and fix it in place with a glue-covered cocktail stick.

POCHIBUKURO
MONEY-GIFT ENVELOPE

In Japan, it was once considered rude to give money unwrapped so this small envelope is used to hold coins or folded bills with which to show one's gratitude. As the *pochibukuro* is now also used to hold money given on special occasions I have made a small *pochibukuro* which could contain coins, stamps, and small gifts. As the back of the paper also appears in the front, it may be nice to use a reversible paper, or two different types of paper pasted together—you can develop your own individual designs.

MATERIAL

◆ **1 sheet of *kyo chiyogami,* 6 x 6 in. (15 x 15cm)**

Difficulty level: 2

1 Make a pair of cross-shaped marker creases. Unfold and find the distance one-third of the way along one crease. Fold the tip over along this line and score the fold.

2 Fold the previously turned tip back to the outside of the piece.

3 Fold the tip back in half once more, ensuring that it is not folded over the center line.

4 Turn the right hand tip over so that it touches the top left edge of the turned bottom tip.

5 Repeat steps 2 and 3 for the left flap.

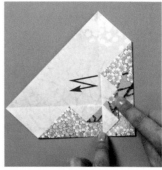

6 Turn the top tip down to the outer edge of the object and repeat steps 2 and 3 once more.

7 Turn the left hand tip over to the far side of the piece, creating a square.

8 Repeat steps 2 and 3 again then lift up and open the bottom so that the left hand side can be tucked in.

9 Flatten and tuck in the flaps so that the final envelope is perfectly symmetrical.

KINPU—MONEY WRAPPER

Japan has a custom of giving gifts of money on special occasions to convey feelings of congratulation, gratitude, or even condolence. The folded envelope used to wrap these gifts of money is called the *kinpu*. It can be made from various designs, but the most important thing to include while you are making your envelope is your feelings. Here, I made a traditional design wrapped with the *mizuhiki* paper ribbon (see pages 82–3). The envelope can also also be used to cover cards, photographs, or paintings—instead of using *mizuhiki*, you might choose to finish the project with ribbons or paper string instead.

MATERIALS

◆ **1 sheet of *taireishi* (red and gilt), 12 x 12 in. (30 x 30cm)**

◆ **1 sheet of white *washi*, 11½ x 11½ in. (29 x 29cm)**

◆ **Glue**

◆ ***Mizuhiki* ribbon**

Difficulty level: 3

1 Paste the white paper onto the reverse side of *taireishi* with a small amount of glue at the four corners. Fold the bottom left corner three-quarters of the way toward its opposite, making a valley fold.

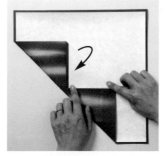

2 Fold the tip of the flap to meet the left edge of the object, making a pleat fold.

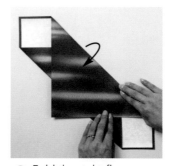

3 Fold the right flap over toward the left, using the pleat fold as the fold line.

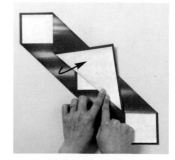

4 Fold the tip of the right flap back along the center line to make a mountain fold.

5 While leaving ⅜ in. (1 cm) for the tip, fold the right flap back on itself to make a pleat fold.

6 After placing the money or gift inside, fold the ends underneath the object.

7 Tie the envelope with the *mizuhiki* and make an *awaji* knot (see pages 82–3).

MIZUHIKI—PAPER RIBBON

Mizuhiki is a colored paper cord used to seal envelopes, the origin of which can be traced back to the sixth century AD, when ambassadors to China returned home with gifts that were tied with red and white twine as a charm against evil. *Mizuhiki* made from twisted washi paper and glue were used long before the custom rose in popularity during the Edo period (1603–1867), becoming more elaborate and gorgeous. It is now an indispensable element of a gift in Japan, and today the design and the type of *mizuhiki* differ according to their usage. This is the most common design, named *awaji musubi* (abalone knot), which is tied around money envelopes.

MATERIALS

◆ *Mizuhiki*

◆ *Kinpu* **ceremony envelope**

◆ **Scissors**

Difficulty level: 4

1 Place the ribbon underneath the envelope with the silver end to the left and the gold to the right. (If you are using the red and white one, then the white part should be on the left.) Bend the *mizuhiki* around the center of the envelope and hold it with your finger.

2 Make a loop with the silver cord and pass the gold cord over the loop and underneath the silver tail.

3 Thread the loose end of the gold cord up through the silver loop from underneath.

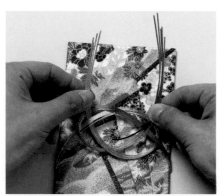

4 Thread the gold end back over itself and immediately underneath the silver loop.

5 Arrange the *awaji* knot into even loops, straightening up both ends of the cord before trimming off any excess with scissors.

CONTEMPORARY
PROJECTS

BENTO-BAKO—LUNCH BOX

This lunch box will surely create wonderful memories for your child's party or picnic. You can make the box any size, according to the paper you have. By simply using two sheets of paper together, you will make a sturdy container that will not lose its shape. Your young guests can take the boxes home as goodie bags and keep on using them to hold trinkets and toys. For this box, I have used the *washi* with a small flower design, which is represented as a plain pink in the artwork over the page, and plain *mingeishi*, which is highlighted in pale green for clarity.

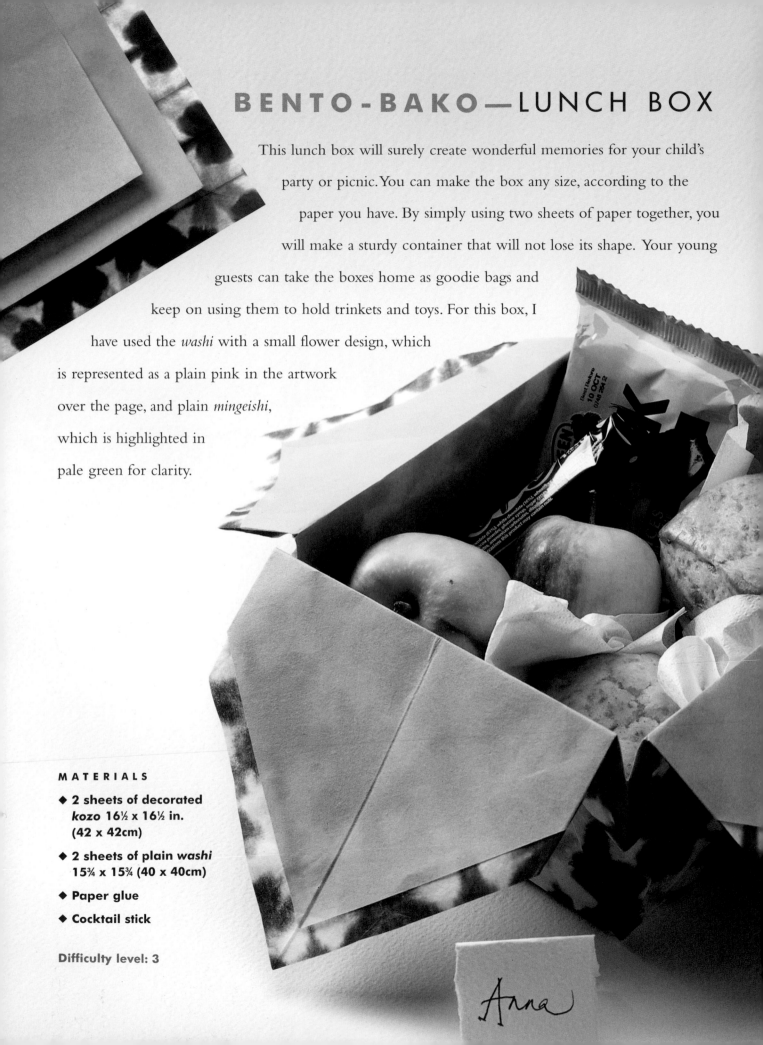

MATERIALS

- **2 sheets of decorated *kozo* 16½ x 16½ in. (42 x 42cm)**
- **2 sheets of plain *washi* 15¾ x 15¾ (40 x 40cm)**
- **Paper glue**
- **Cocktail stick**

Difficulty level: 3

Anna

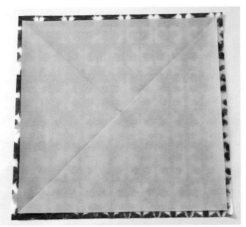

1 Cut two squares of paper: the *kozo* at 16½ in. (42cm) square, the washi at 15¾ in. (40cm) square. Place the decorated washi face down with the plain sheet of *kozo* centered on top.

2 Use a cocktail stick to position a little paper glue at all four corners, fixing the two sheets together.

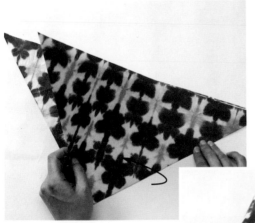

3 Begin by making a square fold (see page 16). Fold one pocket over to make a crease. Unfold and open up the pocket and refold along the crease you just made. Turn over and repeat on the other pockets to make a square.

4 Fold the points of the two free flaps on each side so that they touch at the central fold. Turn over and repeat on the reverse.

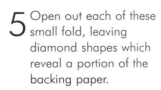

5 Open out each of these small fold, leaving diamond shapes which reveal a portion of the backing paper.

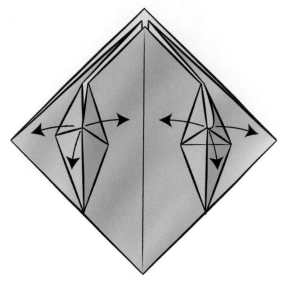

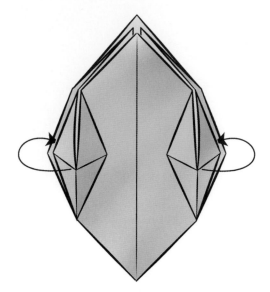

6 Fold all the triangular shape made in the previous step back into the center. Open these folds out and use them as marker creases, pushing down the top part of each fold so that the paper meets along the vertical. Repeat the process on every flap.

7 Make a mountain fold into which the right and left corners corners can be inserted. Repeat on the opposite side.

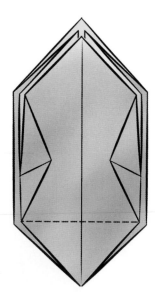

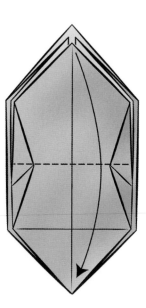

8 Make a crease along the bottom and open it out.

9 Fold the top flap forward, bringing the top point right down to the bottom of the object. Turn over and repeat on the opposite side.

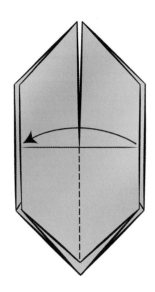
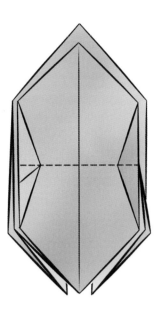

10 Fold the right side to the left and repeat the previous step for all four sides.

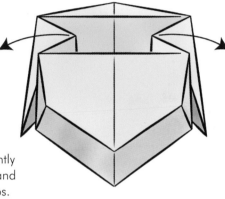

11 Open out the box, gently flattening the bottom and smoothing out the flaps.

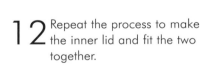

12 Repeat the process to make the inner lid and fit the two together.

KINCHAKU BUKURO
TRIANGLE POUCH

This triangle pouch was designed to mimic the traditional Japanese bag used to carry the kimono, the *kinchaku-bukuro*—which reflected the style and position of its owner in the same way as the kimono itself. Made from a large-sized sheet of *washi*, the small pouch can match different tastes, depending on the design and texture of the paper. Shown here are two pouches, one using *washi* with a chic design for adults, the other a bright, colorful paper for children. Using different types of string or beads to give each pouch its own special character, create a unique pouch using your own sense of style. A useful tip to remember when folding a large sheet of paper is to make the creases as neat and as firm as possible.

MATERIALS

- ◆ **1 sheet of modern *washi*, 24 x 24 in. (60 x 60cm)**
- ◆ **Cardboard sheet 4¾ x 4¾ in. (12 x 12cm)**
- ◆ **Ribbon, or string**
- ◆ **Beads**
- ◆ **Paper punch**
- ◆ **Ruler**
- ◆ **Pencil**

Difficulty level: 4

1 Mark points 4½ in. (11.5cm) from one end and fold along the line. Mark points 4¾ in. (12cm) on from this fold and fold again. Repeat from the other end.

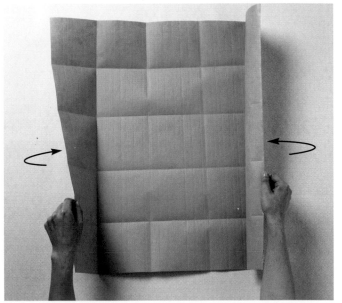

2 Open out the paper and rotate it through 90 degrees. Repeat Step 1, making valley folds.

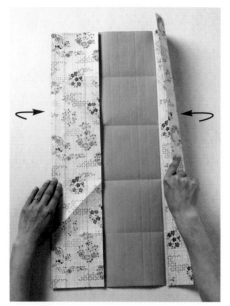

3 Unfold the paper again and make four angled mountain folds for creases between the edge and first crease, as in the photo.

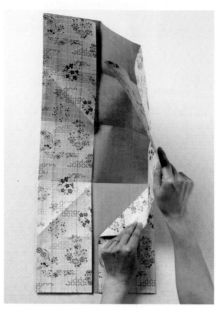

4 Stand both edges up and fold the angled creases marked in step 3, creating mountain folds.

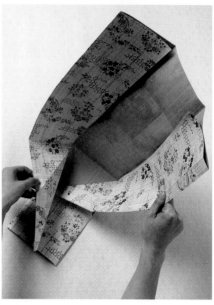

5 Fold over the top edges, tucking them inside.

6 Repeat steps 4 and 5 for the bottom edges. Fold the bottom edges inside to create the basic box shape.

7 Pull the outer flaps up over the box, tuck the ends over the rim, and tuck them in.

8 Create the box's opening by squeezing the two wrapped sides together.

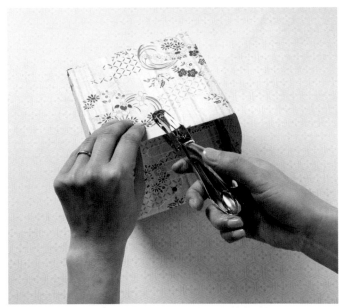

9 Make a hole on both sides ⅝ in. (1.5cm) from the top to lace string through the holes.

10 Place the sheet of cardboard in the bottom of the pouch. Lace the string through a bead first and then lace the string folded in half through the holes.

11 Knot the other end of the string. Lace the knotted end of the string back through the other end with the bead on it, and close the mouth of the bag. Press in the two sides facing each other to form gussets.

HYOSHI—BOOK COVER

Personalize the books in your library by making dust covers that will not only protect them but also make them even more elegant, with this distinctive pleated design. The paper used here is modern Japanese *washi* called *tomohana*—a specially embossed *unryushi* which is very thin with a delicate, silky touch. It has a single colored fiber scattered over its surface to give a background color. Alternatively, include a built-in pocket in your design, where you can keep your rough paper or a bookmark. For the cover on page 97, I have used one sheet of *mingeishi* and one of a translucent, striped *washi*.

MATERIALS

◆ **1 sheet of modern *washi*, 16 x 20 in. (40 x 50cm)**
◆ **Ruler**
◆ **Pencil**

Difficulty level: 2

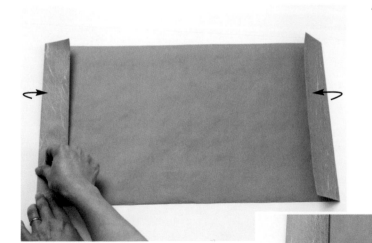

1 Take a piece of paper 4 in. (10cm) longer and 10 in. (25cm) wider then the book you are covering and, placing it face down, turn over each end 2 in. (5cm) to make valley folds.

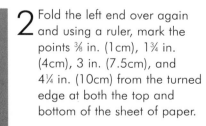

2 Fold the left end over again and using a ruler, mark the points ⅜ in. (1cm), 1¾ in. (4cm), 3 in. (7.5cm), and 4¼ in. (10cm) from the turned edge at both the top and bottom of the sheet of paper.

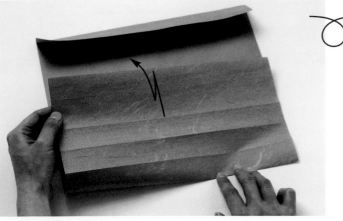

3 Using the ruler, join up the marks with a pencil and make valley folds along the scored lines between the marks.

4 Turn over the paper and create four pleat folds by pinching the paper along the creases you have just made, folding them forward like the knife pleats on a skirt.

5 Turn the paper over again and unfold the crease you made at step 2. Place the book on the paper to mark the positions of the horizontal folds with the pencil.

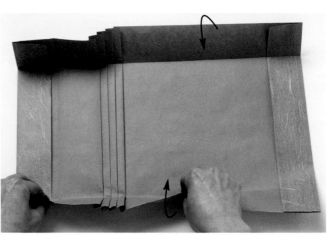

6 Fold over the top and bottom edges.

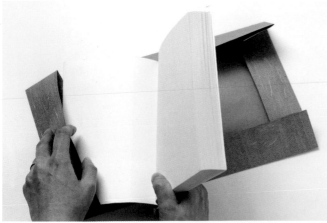

7 Refold the crease you just unfolded at step 5 and insert the book cover.

8 Adjusting for the thickness of the book, fold over the right edge of the paper and insert the back cover likewise.

ALTERNATIVE DESIGN

MATERIALS

◆ **2 sheets of thin *washi* (*tengujoshi* and *mingeishi*), or a sheet of reversible paper 12 x 13 in. (30 x 33cm)**

◆ **Ruler**

◆ **Pencil**

Adjust the size of paper to match the book you are covering.

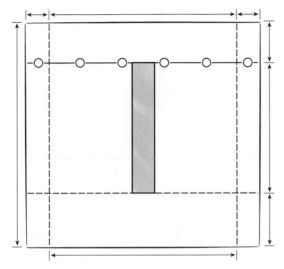

1 Put two sheets of paper together and mark and fold the vertical and horizontal folds as shown in the diagram. Fold over the paper to make a valley fold where it will form a pocket.

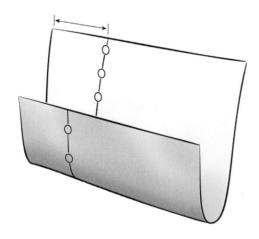

2 Fold at the point 2 in. (5cm) from the right edge to make a mountain fold and turn the paper over.

3 Insert the front cover into the left pocket. Adjust for the thickness of your book and fold over the right edge, inserting the back cover likewise.

ORIGAMI CARD—GREETINGS CARD

If you make this greetings card with colorful paper, it will be perfect to give for a birthday or with a congratulatory gift. The crane is auspicious in Japan and is a symbol of longevity. One thousand *origami* cranes are frequently sent to the sick to pray for recovery from illness and for long life. So, I suggest using the crane to decorate congratulations cards as well as get-well cards. Your original handmade card adds heartfelt love to the words inside.

MATERIALS/FAN

◆ **A5 card stock**

◆ *Kyo-chiyogami* **(A) for fan 6 x 3 in.
(15 x 7.5cm)**

◆ **Plain** *washi* **lining (B) 6 x 6 in.
(15 x 15cm)**

◆ **2 pieces of gold** *mizuhiki* **6 in.
(15 cm)**

◆ **Paper cutter**

◆ **Ruler**

◆ **Glue**

◆ **Pencil**

Difficulty level: 3

1 To make the fan, fold in *washi* A ¼ in. (5mm) from both edges, and make pleat folds of ⅜ in. (1cm) width, creating an appearance like a concertina.

2 Fold *washi* B in half, and paste it on the card stock making the center of the washi and card stock meet each other. Apply the glue sparingly in spots as needed—too much glue may make the paper wrinkle.

3 Apply glue on both edges of the fan made in step 1, and paste it onto the center of *washi* B.

4 Attach the mizuhiki knotted in an *awaji musubi* (abalone knot).

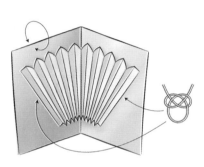

MATERIALS/CRANES

◆ **A5 card stock**

◆ **Paper cutter**

◆ **2 sheets of** *edo-chiyogami* **6 x 6 in.
(15 x 15cm) and 2½ x 2½ in. (6 x 6cm)**

◆ **3 sheets of diamond-shape** *mingeishi*
1½ x 1½ in. (3.5 x 3.5cm)

◆ **Ruler**

◆ **Glue**

Difficulty level: 3

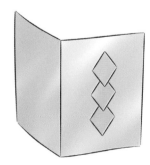

1 Paste three small diamond-shaped colored washi onto the center of the front of the card stock.

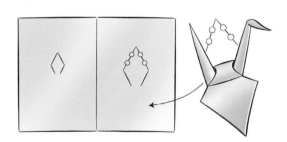

2 Make a pair of cranes, one small and one large. (see pages 22–25). Paste one side of the wing of the large crane inside the card to the right of the center fold and cut around the outline of the wing so as to form a triangle when opened.

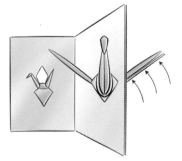

3 Paste one side of the wing of the small crane to the front of the card and repeat on the other side for the large crane.

KAZARIZURU—FANTAIL CRANE

At New Year in Japan, houses and rooms are prepared with special decorations. Like Christmas in the West, families come together, and celebrate the festival with special food. I made this fantail crane with gold and red reversible paper for a New Year's decoration. If you fold it using patterned paper of European design, you can create a pretty ornament. If you fold it with a small sheet of paper, for a chopstick rest, then it will be a suitable decoration for a party table. It may look difficult at first, but the simple repetition of the folding will just enhance your enjoyment of paper folding. Use medium-thick paper and make the creases accurately in order to give an elegant finish.

MATERIALS

◆ **One sheet of reversible paper 9½ x 9½ in. (24 x 24cm)**

Difficulty level: 5

1 Begin with the square fold (see page 16) and then fold the front flaps to meet in the center.

2 Fold the bottom triangle up to make a crease.

3 Unfold all three scored creases. Raise, open and flatten the front flaps.

4 Turn the object over onto its back. Fold the right flap over, to cover the left.

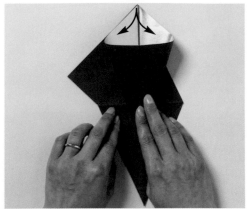

5 Open up the flap you just folded to the left, and flatten it. Open up the left flap and flatten this in the same way.

6 Fold the top face of both flaps to the center and make creases.

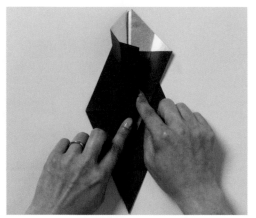

7 Open up the left flap, flatten, and crease.

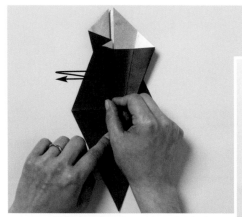

8 Turn the flap you have just folded back to the left along the center line and make a pleat fold. Open the unfolded right side and repeat the crease and pleat fold.

9 Open the flaps as in the photo and count out an even number of creases on each side.

10 Fold the triangle in the middle up.

11 Fold the paper in half lengthwise and make a crease.

12 Unfold the object and while holding the fantail piece with the right hand, fold the left part back along the crease you made in step 10 to make a valley fold.

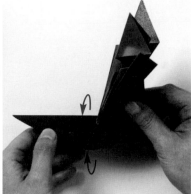

13 Make a crease at the middle of the left part. Unfold it and make an inside fold to form the bird's neck.

14 Make an inside fold at the tip to make the crane's head. Spread the wings and arrange the form of the crane.

USAGI—RABBIT

The image of a white rabbit is a favorite in Japan and frequently appears in ancient Japanese tales and folklore. One of the most traditional images in Japan is a rabbit on the moon, pounding rice cake with a pestle and mortar. Here, I made a white rabbit with white *washi* paper, reminiscent of the folklore. It may seem difficult to fold at first, but after much practice, you will make it with no trouble. Use different sizes of paper to make a rabbit family. Alternatively, you can use sheets of patterned paper to make a colorful grouping.

MATERIALS

◆ **White *kozo* in two sizes 10 x 10 in. (25.5 x 25.5cm) and 6 x 6 in. (15 x 15cm)**

◆ **Scissors**

Difficulty level: 5

1 Begin with the square fold (see page 16), creasing accurately.

2 Fold the front right and left flaps to the center. Fold the bottom triangle up and make three creases.

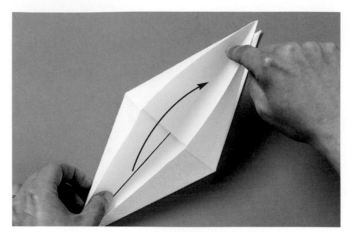

3 Unfold into the square. Raise and open the front flap, pulling it down before flattening it.

4 Repeat these steps on the reverse side to leave the object in a long diamond shape.

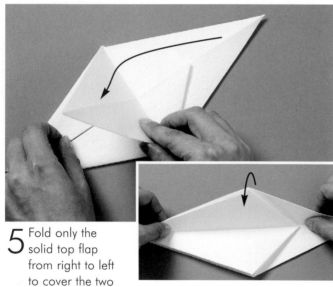

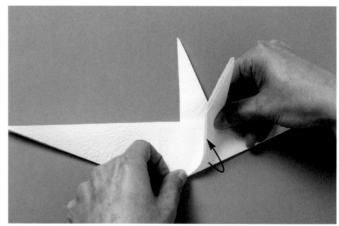

5 Fold only the solid top flap from right to left to cover the two long arms. Then, fold the upper flap over to make a long, thin triangle.

6 Fold the top arm of the three piled flaps at right angles to the object about ⅜ in. (1cm) from the center. Turn over and also fold up the bottom flap.

7 Pick the object up and, after turning it over, fold the center flap along the crease already made for the top and bottom flaps to make a marker crease. Open out the object and refold it back on itself so that the top and bottom flaps are now enclosed.

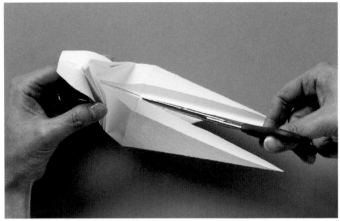

8 Pull down two-thirds of the enclosing flap that you just made in step 7. Then, make an inside fold half way up the flap you just pulled out, to make the rabbit's nose.

9 Open out the object and cut along the center line to the crease in the middle. Be careful not to cut the bottom sheet.

10 Take the top flap you just cut and bring it the left, folding it under itself to make a mountain fold.

11 Again, fold the same flap under itself in the middle. Crease the tip of the foot and fold inside. Repeat these steps on the other side.

12 Make a pleat fold for the tail. Unfold and turn it inside along the first crease, pulling out the tip at the second crease. Arrange the form.

SAKURA ZARA
PLATE OF CHERRY BLOSSOM

The *sakura*, or cherry, is a special tree that has charmed the Japanese since ancient times. In spring, the cherry trees blossom throughout the country, covering the land with flower petals. I made this lovely plate by combining five petals folded from separate sheets of *taireishi* into the shape. A different type of *washi* would produce an entirely different effect. If you make the dish with rich, gorgeous paper, it can be used at a party, while a plate made from chic plain paper would be perfect as a small container in the bedroom.

MATERIAL:

◆ **5 sheets of colored *taireishi*, 5 x 5 in. (12 x 12cm)**

◆ **Glue**

◆ **Cocktail stick**

Difficulty level: 3

1 Fold the paper in half to make a horizontal crease in the middle of the paper. Unfold and fold the left and right sides into the center to make creases.

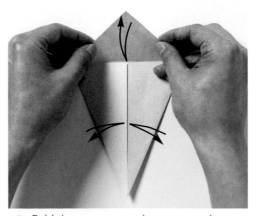

2 Fold the top corner down, using the folded flaps as the crease mark, to form a triangle.

3 Open the flaps out, folding the far end inside, then turn both sides over so that what were the short ends of the flaps meet together along the center line.

4 Halve the object by folding the right-hand side back underneath to the reverse side.

5 Fold the bottom triangle of paper away from you, making a crease along the edge of the flap.

6 Open out the top flap and fold the bottom edge up, inserting it into the upper triangle.

7 Fold back the flap you just opened in step 6, then use its far edge as the crease line to turn over the exposed triangle.

8 Push the top triangle through the middle to make an inside fold. Make a crease at the bottom as shown in the photo.

9 To open out the petal, start by flattening out the triangular part of the object.

10 Carefully open out the object to form the final shape of the petal.

11 Make four more petals. Using a toothpick, place glue around their pointed ends and fit them together to make the plate.

MARU UTSUWA—DISH

This design for an open container is possible by first making accurate creases, and then forming the paper into a multi-dimensional shape that's similar to the one you made for the *tato*. The essential tip is to make neat and accurate creases. With different designs and sizes of paper, you can make dishes with different qualities, possibly even from thick paper, depending upon how you intend to use them. Your guests might find it difficult to believe that they are made from only a single piece of paper.

MATERIALS

◆ **1 sheet of *kyo chiyogami***
8½ x 8½ in. (22 x 22cm)

Difficulty level: 4

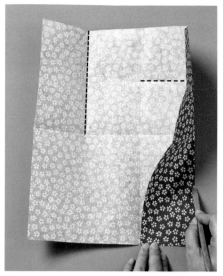

1 Begin with the paper's plain side upward. First make cross-shaped creases, then add quarter creases to all four squares. Unfold.

2 Fold in half to make a rectangle and fold the top flap forward on the diagonal to make a valley fold. Turn over and repeat on the other side. Unfold and fold in half the other way, and repeat making diagonal creases on both sides.

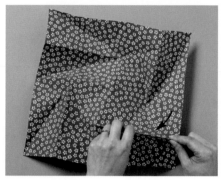

3 Unfold and place the paper face up. Pinch the quarter crease to make a mountain fold.

4 Fold along the outer part of the diagonal crease to make a valley fold.

5 Hold each of these flaps together and fold them outward.

6 Repeat folding along the creases for all four sides to shape the paper into three dimensions.

7 Tuck the flaps you have lifted behind the folds to form the shape of the dish.

KODOMO BOSHI—CHILD'S HAT

One of the fun things about paper folding is creating new pieces from old or used papers. Here, an old sheet of gift wrap has been used to make a child's hat. Of course, it is also fun to make a balloon (see page 34) or a *samurai* helmet (see page 38), but this child's hat is simple to make. It can be used as a party hat for adults as well as for children. It is preferable to use thin but strong and untearable paper, though you could also make it with old newspaper.

MATERIALS
◆ **1 sheet of *momiwashi*
21½ x 21½ in.
(55 x 55 cm) for a child,
26 x 26 in.
(65 x 65cm) for adults**

Difficulty level: 1

1 Fold the paper in half to make a triangle then bring the right corner across to the other side of the object making a horizontal edge.

2 Take the left corner across to match.

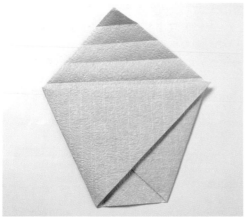

3 Fold the front flap down in four equal sections to make creases.

4 Fold the front flap down from the top along the creases one by one then turn over and repeat.

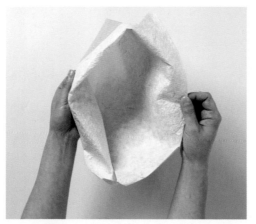

5 Holding in the edges gently ease the hat open.

6 Press the top in to create the final shape of the hat.

KASHI ZARA—TEA PLATE

There are many varieties of tea plates made from many different materials, including porcelain, earthenware, wood, and lacquer, to name but a few. Here, I have made a tea plate with modern, patterned *chiyogami*. It is ideal for serving Japan's traditional dry candy, *higashi*, but you could treat your guests to chocolate or cookies if you prefer. Why not make it as a centerpiece for a tea party or a children's party; you'll be sure to be creating conversation too.

MATERIALS

◆ **1 sheet of modern *chiyogami* 7 x 7 in. (18 x 18cm)**

Difficulty level: 2

1 Begin with the triangle fold (see page 17) and then fold the corners of the front flap up to the top to make triangle creases.

2 Open up the lefthand triangle to make a square and repeat on the opposite side.

3 Fold both the right and left flaps of the square toward each other at the center of the square to make creases. Raise, open and flatten the left hand flap to make a petal in a long bamboo-leaf shape.

4 Repeat the previous step on the opposite side.

5 Place the petal along the center line, making a pleat fold underneath.

6 Turn the corners up toward the center and make square folds on both sides.

7 Use the same method as in steps 3 and 4 to make the outer petals.

DENKIGASA—LAMPSHADE

Handmade *washi* has been used in Japan for centuries for illumination in the form of various types of lanterns, and the paper and pattern display their charms exquisitely when wrapped round a lamp. *Washi* is also still used in sliding paper screens and sliding doors, which are musts for any truly Japanese-style room. *Kyokarakami*, and handmade *unryushi* in particular, which are thin but robust, are also used throughout the modern Japanese interior. Take care with this project; only use reputable ready-made light fittings and very low-wattage bulbs, and never allow the paper to touch a lit bulb.

MATERIALS

- ◆ **1 sheet of *kyokarakami* 20 x 14 in. (50 x 35cm)**
- ◆ **Wooden embroidery hoop, diameter 6 in. (15cm)**
- ◆ **Cork board or coasters 6 x 6 x ⅝ in. (15 x 15 x 1.5cm)**
- ◆ **Small, ready-made light fitting**
- ◆ **Light bulb (20w or 40w)**
- ◆ **Three pieces of bamboo, ½–⅝ in. (1.2–1.5cm) thick**
- ◆ **Screws**
- ◆ **Screwdriver**
- ◆ **Glue**

Difficulty level: 2

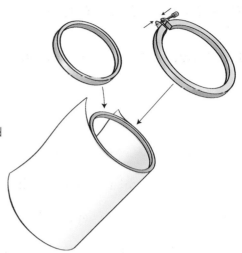

1 Take apart the outer and inner hoop. Loosen the clasp of the hoop.

2 Gently wind the *washi* onto the hoop, fixing it with a little glue. The pattern of the paper should be near the bottom of the lamp.

3 When the paper is neatly wound, apply the outer hoop and fix the paper in place with glue.

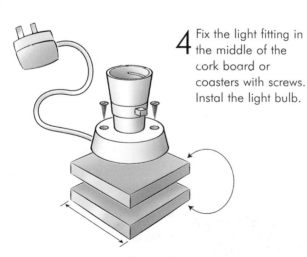

4 Fix the light fitting in the middle of the cork board or coasters with screws. Instal the light bulb.

5 Cover the bulb with the lampshade assembled in step 3. Be certain to keep the socket assembly in the center of the lampshade. Place three pieces of bamboo under the lampshade and run the electric cord out between the bamboo feet. Never allow the paper to touch a lit bulb.

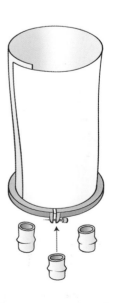

KAMIBANA — TISSUE-PAPER FLOWER

This artificial flower reminds all Japanese people of childhood
events and youthful days at school sports festivals or the summer
festival, *hanagasa odori,* and now also the Star Festival. Although
very simple to make, this peony gives a lifelike impression and
with thin paper, you can make a very elegant flower.
Either make the entire flower with the same
colored paper, or use a different color for the
center. Here, I have made flowers using alternate
colored papers. You can make lovely flowers with
any size of paper.

MATERIALS

◆ **3 sheets of *unryushi* or *rakusuishi* 4 x 5 in. (10 x 12cm)**

◆ **3 sheets of tissue paper 4 x 5 in. (10 x 12cm)**

◆ **Thin wire or thread**

◆ **Scissors**

Difficulty level: 1

1 Make a pile of six sheets of paper with tissue first and then washi, one after the other. Fold the paper in half and make a crease in the center.

2 Turn the pile through 90 degrees and make repeated valley and mountain folds at ¼ in. (5mm) intervals, creating a pile like an accordion.

3 Tie the center of the folded paper with wire or thread, leaving long lengths at both ends.

4 Spread both edges and cut around the edges at a smooth angle.

5 Gently pull each piece of paper up toward the center of the flower, separating each sheet of paper from the other, taking care not to tear them.

6 Arrange the form of the flower by evening out the form of the peony.

AJISAI KAKEJIKU
TAPESTRY WITH HYDRANGEA

First prepare the tapestry base from thick, handmade *washi*. Leave a space of about ½–¾ in. (1.5–2cm) at the top and bottom of the *washi* for the glue to attach it to a wooden dowel or bamboo as a tapestry rod so that you could roll it up. Here, I have patterned the tapestry with hydrangea flowers, or *ajisai*. You can apply any *origami* model in the place of the hydrangea used here—try making your own unique tapestry.

MATERIALS

- ◆ *Washi* tapestry 16 x 12 in. (40 x 30cm)
- ◆ Small flowers: 30 pieces of *kozo* paper 1 x 1 in. (2.5 x 2.5cm)
- ◆ Large flowers: 10 pieces of *kozo* paper 1¼ x 1¼ in. (3 x 3cm)
- ◆ Leaves: 2 pieces of *kozo* paper 3½ x 3½ in. (8.5 x 8.5cm)

- ◆ Glue
- ◆ Cocktail stick
- ◆ *Mizuhiki*

Difficulty level: 3

MAKING THE FLOWERS

1 Place the white side of the paper face up and make a diagonal crease. Unfold and score, then repeat for the opposite corners. Fold the sheet in half twice, creating a square.

2 Squeeze the paper together into a cross shape and flatten onto the table. It is easier to make a square fold this way with a small piece of paper.

3 Fold the front flaps to the center. Repeat for the reverse side.

4 Fold the bottom corner up to the top point and make a score fold.

5 Holding the long point, pull the ends apart to open the top flaps, flattening the flower. Make 40 of them.

MAKING THE LEAVES

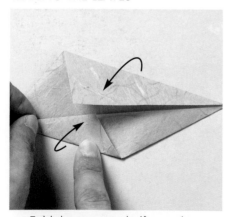

1 Fold the paper in half to make a triangle. Unfold and fold the top and bottom corners to the center. Fold the left corners to the center.

2 Fold the right tip downward and score—the angle of this fold determines the shape of the leaf.

3 Turn the point back on itself so that it lies along the center of the leaf.

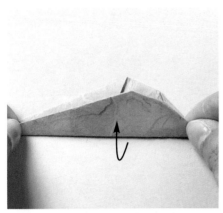

4 Fold in half along the center line to make a valley fold.

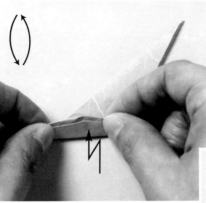

5 Rotate the paper 180 degrees and fold the left tip ¼ in. (5mm) from the edge at an angle of 20 degrees and continue making pleat folds along the length of the leaf.

6 Unfold the pleats and open the object out into the leaf shape created earlier.

7 Paste the leaves and flowers onto the tapestry. Balance the whole picture; take care not to put too many flowers on top of each other.

SUPPLIERS

Special thanks to all the suppliers who kindly supplied materials for this book. The author unreservedly recommends them.

SUGIHARA WASHIPAPER INC.
17-2, Oizu, Echizen-shi,
Fukui 915-0235
Japan
Fax: +81-778-42-0144
e-mail:sugihara@washiya.com
www.washiya.com/washinomokuji/
english.html

KARACHO STUDIO (Shugakuin)
36-9 Mizukawaracho, Shugakuin,
Sakyo-ku, Kyoto 606-8027
Japan
Tel: +81-75-721-4422
Fax: +81-75-721-4430
e-mail: mailto@karacho.co.jp
www.karacho.co.jp

AWAGAMI FACTORY
136 Kawahigashi, Yamakawa-cho,
Yoshinogawa-shi,
Tokushima 779-3401
Japan
Tel: +81-883-42-2035
Fax: +81-883-42-6085
e-mail: info@awagami.or.jp
www.awagami.or.jp

INTERNATIONAL ORIGAMI CENTER
Yushimano Kobayashi Corporation
(Origami Kaikan), 1-7-4 Yushima,
Bunkyo-ku, Tokyo 113-0034
Japan
Tel: +81-3-3811-4025
Fax: +81-3-3815-3348
e-mail: admin@origamikaikan.co.jp
www.origamikaikan.co.jp/origami/
e_frame.html

WAGAMI-DO
4-33-6 Hakusan Bunkyo-ku,
Tokyo 112-0001
Japan
Tel: +81-3-3813-7117
Fax: +81-3-3813-8299
e-mail: wagami@cna.ne.jp
www.cna.ne.jp/~wagami/index.htm

ONAO LTD.
184-3 Takata Taisho,
Ichikawadaimon-cho,
Nishiyatsushiro-gun,
Yamanashi 409-3606
Japan
Tel: +81-55-272-0321
Fax: +81-55-272-0323
e-mail: info@onao.co.jp
www.onao.co.jp

KAMIYAKATA SHIMAYU LTD.
2-4-25 Ote, Matsumoto-shi,
Nagano 390-0874
Japan
Tel: +81-263-35-1000
Fax: +81-263-36-6554
e-mail: info@shimayu.co.jp
www.shimayu.co.jp

USEFUL BOOKS AND WEBSITES

Special thanks to the origami artists and creators who consented to their inclusion in this book (see page 128.).

BOOKS
Kazuo Kobayashi *Fun with Origami* (Kodansha International Ltd.);
    Origami Zakka Book (Bunka Publishing Bureau);
    Kantan Origami 100 (Nihon Vogue-Sha Co. Ltd.)
Rika Masahisa *Origami Zakka—12 Months of Origami
    Sundries* (Kawade Shobo Shinsha Publishers)
Nick Robinson *The Encyclopedia of Origami Techniques*
    (Search Press Ltd.)

ENGLISH-LANGUAGE WEBSITES
Round R, Rika Masahisa: www.round-r.com
Japan Origami Academic Society: www.origami.gr.jp
Nippon Origami Association: www.origami-noa.com
British Origami Society: www.britishorigami.org.uk

JAPANESE-LANGUAGE WEBSITES
Origami Kyoshitsu: www.asahi-net.or.jp/~uz4s-
mrym/page/origami0.html
Origami Club: www.origami-club.com
Wanokurashi: www.japanism.net
Explantae: www007.upp.so-net.ne.jp/xpl/explantae.htm

MATERIALS DIRECTORY
Please contact me if you have difficulty purchasing any of the
Japanese papers used in this book, or cannot contact the
information sources mentioned above. Also, if you should
have any queries, please do not hesitate to ask at the
following site, where I will be very happy to assist:
    www.asahi-net.or.jp/~HH5Y-SZK/ono/atelier.htm

INDEX

ACKNOWLEDGMENTS

No book is written alone. This achievement represents the sum of the generous help and co-operation given by family, friends, and many others. My special thanks go to Yukiko Tagawa for translating my draft; to Chizuko Tokuno, Natsuko Watanabe, Mr. Hiroaki Takai, Mr. Fumiaki Shingu, and Mr. Tsutomu Nakai for much useful advice; to Michael Herbstler for proofreading; to Mr. and Mrs. Hancock and their son, Thomas; to the Deerhurst & Apperley C of E School, and the staff of the National Trust shop at Polesden Lacey in Surrey for their sincere co-operation; and to Mr. Yasuyuki Suzuki for creating my website. Thanks also to Georgina Harris, Cindy Richards, and Robin Gurdon for editing; to Geoff Dann for taking photos; to Christine Wood for designing this book; to Masaharu and Yoko Ono, my parents at home in Japan for their continued support; and finally to my son Roshin, for acting as the model for the child's hat and for all his other support.

I also thank all those who were involved in publishing this book, and all the readers of this book for being interested in Japanese papercrafts and Japanese traditional culture.

My biggest thanks go, as usual, to my husband Takumasa for his continued encouragement, always useful suggestions, comments, and help.

ORIGAMI DESIGN CREDITS
Special thanks to the origami artists and creators who consented to the inclusion of their original designs in this book:

Page 30 Based on a unit by Mitsunobu Sonobe / Page 50 Shunzo Amano / Pages 62, 90, 94,114 Rika Masahisa /Page 100 Toshio Chino / Page 108 Mitsue Nakano / Page 112 Nick Robinson.